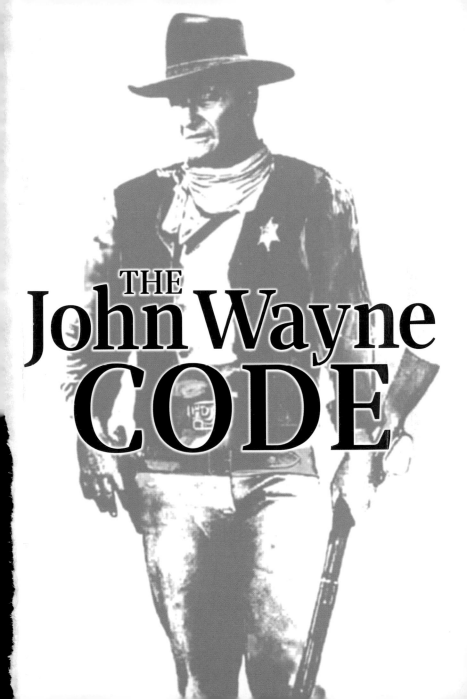

THE
John Wayne
CODE

John Wayne in
Chisum (1970).

People respect my father not just for his classic films, but because John Wayne stands for something beyond entertainment. The values he embodied both on the big screen and in his personal life remind us of what it means to be a man. In the following pages, you'll find my father's words of wisdom, stories about his life and insights that make up the John Wayne Code—an inspiration for us all in our daily lives.

—ETHAN WAYNE

Duke in *Rio Bravo* (1954).

TABLE OF CONTENTS

John Wayne and his friend Ward Bond in *The Wings of Eagles* (1957). The two had been pals since they played football together at USC.

Loyalty

DUKE ALWAYS DID RIGHT BY
THOSE HE LOVED.

John Wayne (hanging off the train to the top left) with members of the cast and crew of *McLintock!* (1963), including Maureen O'Hara (also holding on to the train).

"He is cursed with one failing, his loyalty to friends. And it has cost him many sad moments and many happy moments. But he will never cease to be loyal, ever."

—MAUREEN O'HARA
Duke's friend and frequent costar

Duke with children Melinda, Patrick, Toni and Michael at the Los Angeles Sheriff's Rodeo, early 1950s.

"I have tried to live my life so that my family would love me and my friends respect me. The others can do whatever the hell they please."

—JOHN WAYNE

"Duke's generosity and loyalty stood out in a city rarely known for either. When a friend needed work, that person went on his payroll. When a friend needed help, Duke's wallet was open."

—RONALD REAGAN
former actor and President of the United States

Duke with comedian
Bob Hope and
Ronald Reagan.

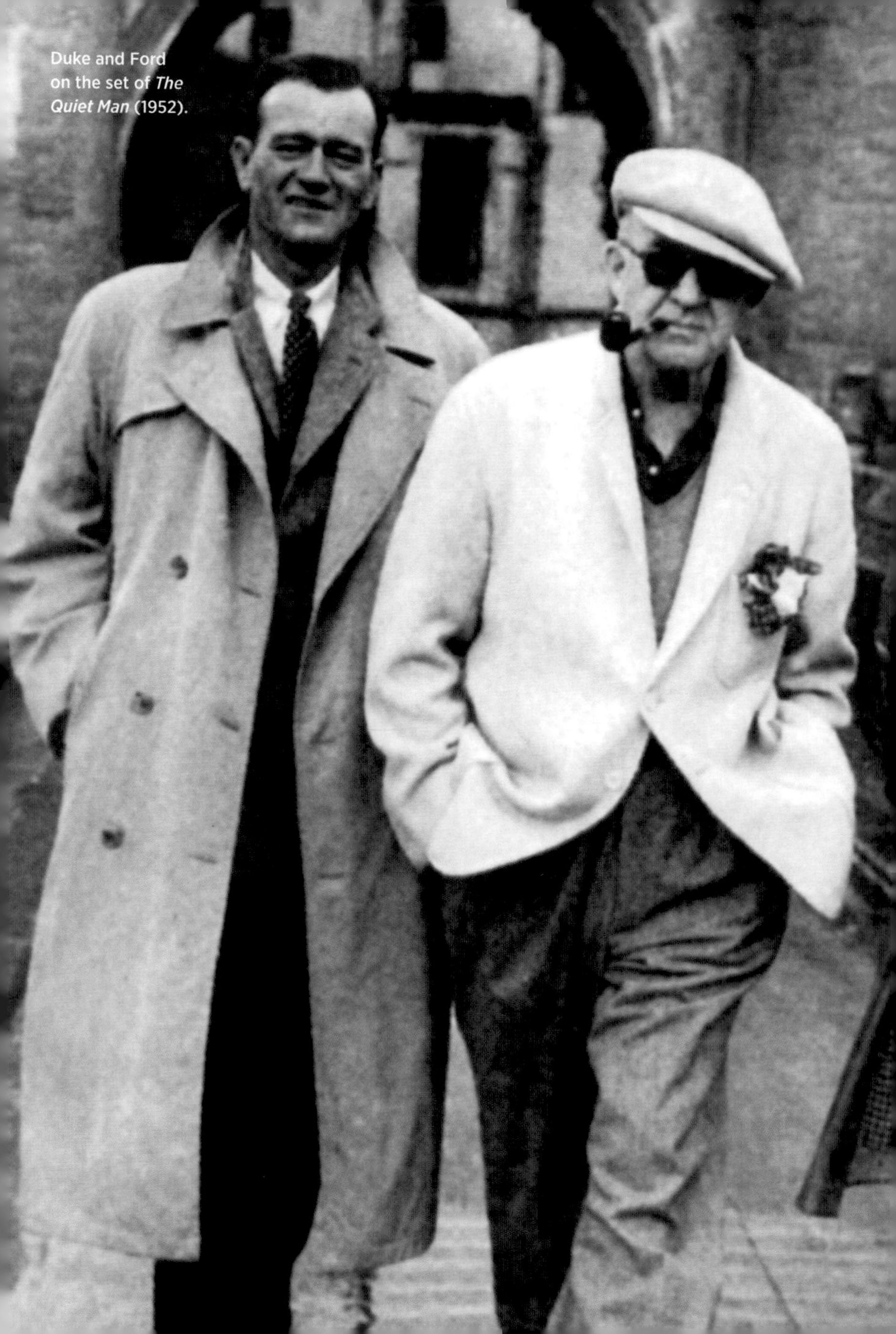

Duke and Ford on the set of *The Quiet Man* (1952).

★

A decade before *The Quiet Man* was released, dynamic duo John Wayne and director John Ford shook hands and made a promise to make that movie in Ireland someday. However, Ford was turned down and told by producers that it was a "silly Irish story that wouldn't make a penny." But Duke knew how badly his mentor wanted to make this film, so he convinced his studio, Republic Pictures, to make *The Quiet Man* under the agreement that Ford, John Wayne and Maureen O'Hara would make a Western as well. This agreement was fulfilled with the making of *Rio Grande*.

* LOYALTY *

As long as people want to pay money to see me act, I'll keep on making Westerns until the day I die.

—JOHN WAYNE

Duke took a great amount of pleasure in the time he spent aboard the *Wild Goose,* his yacht, and consequently felt a fierce loyalty toward the crew who kept his home on the water running smoothly. At the top of that list was Pete Stein, the *Goose*'s skipper, who landed in hot water when Duke's boat scraped a yacht while en route to Catalina Island. When the yacht's owner wrote a letter to Duke complaining of what he felt was Stein's "arrogant" attitude during the aftermath of the accident, John Wayne stuck to his guns and backed Stein in a strongly worded response.

John Wayne aboard the *Wild Goose* with (from left) daughter Marisa, sons Ethan and Patrick, and the boat's captain Pete Stein.

John Wayne and writer James Edward Grant on the set of *Angel and the Badman* (1947).

ohn Wayne commanded more than enough fame to have the rest of Hollywood scrambling to work with him, but Duke always stayed loyal to the men and women who helped him shine brightest on the silver screen. In addition to director and mentor John Ford, with whom he made 14 feature films, John Wayne consistently worked with friend and screenwriter James Edward Grant (who worked on films such as *Angel and the Badman* and *Sands of Iwo Jima*) and costume designer Luster Bayless (the genius behind Duke's iconic looks starting with *McLintock!*). These two individuals, in addition to others, could always count on Duke to reward their hard work with another job offer from the legend.

John Wayne behind the camera on the set of *The Alamo* (1960).

"I've worked in a business where it's almost a requirement to break your word if you want to survive, but whenever I signed a contract for five years or for a certain amount of money, I've always lived up to it."

—JOHN WAYNE

Duke threw his support behind many of the most prominent Republicans of his day, including Barry Goldwater, Richard Nixon and Ronald Reagan, but Duke's loyalty to country always came first. When Jimmy Carter won the presidential election of 1976, Duke telegraphed the former peanut farmer, "Congratulations, sir, from one of the loyal opposition." It was a heartfelt sentiment from the man who never forgot an American's duty was to rise above petty differences and remember the values binding us together.

Duke always had the
courage to follow
the course of his
convictions and never
let petty politics get in
the way of doing what
he felt was right.

"All battles are fought by scared men who'd rather be someplace else."

—AS REAR ADMIRAL ROCKWELL TORREY

In Harm's Way

Duke in *In Harm's Way* (1965).

Richard Widmark
and John Wayne in
The Alamo (1960).

"There's right and there's wrong. Y'gotta do one or the other. You do the one and you're living. Do the other and you may be walking around, but you're dead as a beaver hat."

—AS DAVY CROCKETT
The Alamo

Self-Reliance

JOHN WAYNE WAS A LEGEND OF HIS OWN MAKING.

John Wayne in a scene from *The Cowboys* (1972).

Duke with his
youngest son, Ethan.

REMEMBERING THE LEGEND

"I think he did a lot of things that created responsibility for a young person. Back in the day there were chores every day. When you woke up, there were chores. If you were on the boat, there were chores. If you were on location, there were chores. You'd wake up, and you'd mop the decks and wipe down the rails. And if my father and his friends went fishing, I would have to clean all the fish. If they caught a lot, I'd be gutting fish for hours."

—ETHAN WAYNE
Duke's youngest son

"Sorry don't get it done, Dude."

—AS JOHN T. CHANCE
Rio Bravo

Ricky Nelson and
John Wayne in
Rio Bravo (1959).

"There was one instance on the boat where he kept telling me to pick up my room. I had clothes all over the floor. And after asking me about five times, I woke up to him throwing everything overboard. I learned my lesson. It all came down to disrespect, and in his mind it was disrespectful that I wasn't picking up after myself. That was the only time where I felt the punishment was harder on him than me."

—MARISA WAYNE
Duke's youngest daughter

John Wayne
holds his
youngest, Marisa.

Duke (left) with
his younger
brother, Robert.

TRUE TALL TALES

ohn Wayne made his mark on history by playing some of cinema's most rugged individualists. It helped that he had life experiences to draw on, such as the time he spent as a boy living on a homestead in California's Mojave Desert. Duke would get out of bed well before dawn to help his father with chores around the farm, and then ride a pony named Jenny into town for school.

Duke in *3 Godfathers* (1948).

"I would like to be remembered, well...the Mexicans have a phrase, 'Feo fuerte y formal.' Which means he was ugly, strong and had dignity."

—JOHN WAYNE

I won't be wronged. I won't be insulted. I won't be laid a hand on. I don't do these things to other people, and I require the same from them."

—AS J.B. BOOKS
The Shootist

Duke in
The Shootist
(1976).

★

uke didn't just land at the top of the marquee when he started his movie career. The actor spent nearly a decade climbing the ranks, starring in short, by-the-numbers Westerns made on Hollywood's "Poverty Row." The actors appearing in these films didn't have the luxury of trailers or a crew of wardrobe and makeup experts to get them ready for set. Duke often spent early mornings before a shoot in his car, applying his own makeup to get ready for another day at work.

John Wayne
in a still from
*Overland Stage
Raiders* (1938).

Laurence Harvey, Richard Widmark, and John Wayne in a scene from *The Alamo* (1960).

★

or more than a decade, Duke harbored a dream to bring the story of the Battle of the Alamo to the big screen. When the studio heads refused to give Duke the creative control he felt necessary to do the heroes of the Alamo justice, John Wayne took matters into his own hands. He founded his own production company, Batjac, and labored for years assembling the perfect team for his pet project. In 1960, his initiative bore fruit when *The Alamo* premiered in San Antonio, Texas, another goal the legend accomplished thanks to his belief in himself.

"Out here, a man settles his own problems."

—AS TOM DONIPHON
The Man Who Shot Liberty Valance

Duke in *The Man Who Shot Liberty Valance* (1962).

Duke in *The Cowboys* (1972).

"Courage is being scared to death but saddling up anyway."

—JOHN WAYNE

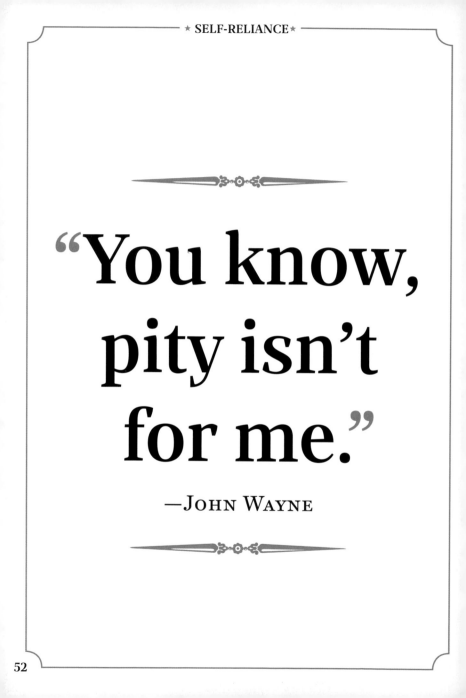

"You know, pity isn't for me."

—JOHN WAYNE

Duke in *The Cowboys* (1972).

Grit

THE DIDN'T COME
TOUGHER THAN DUKE.

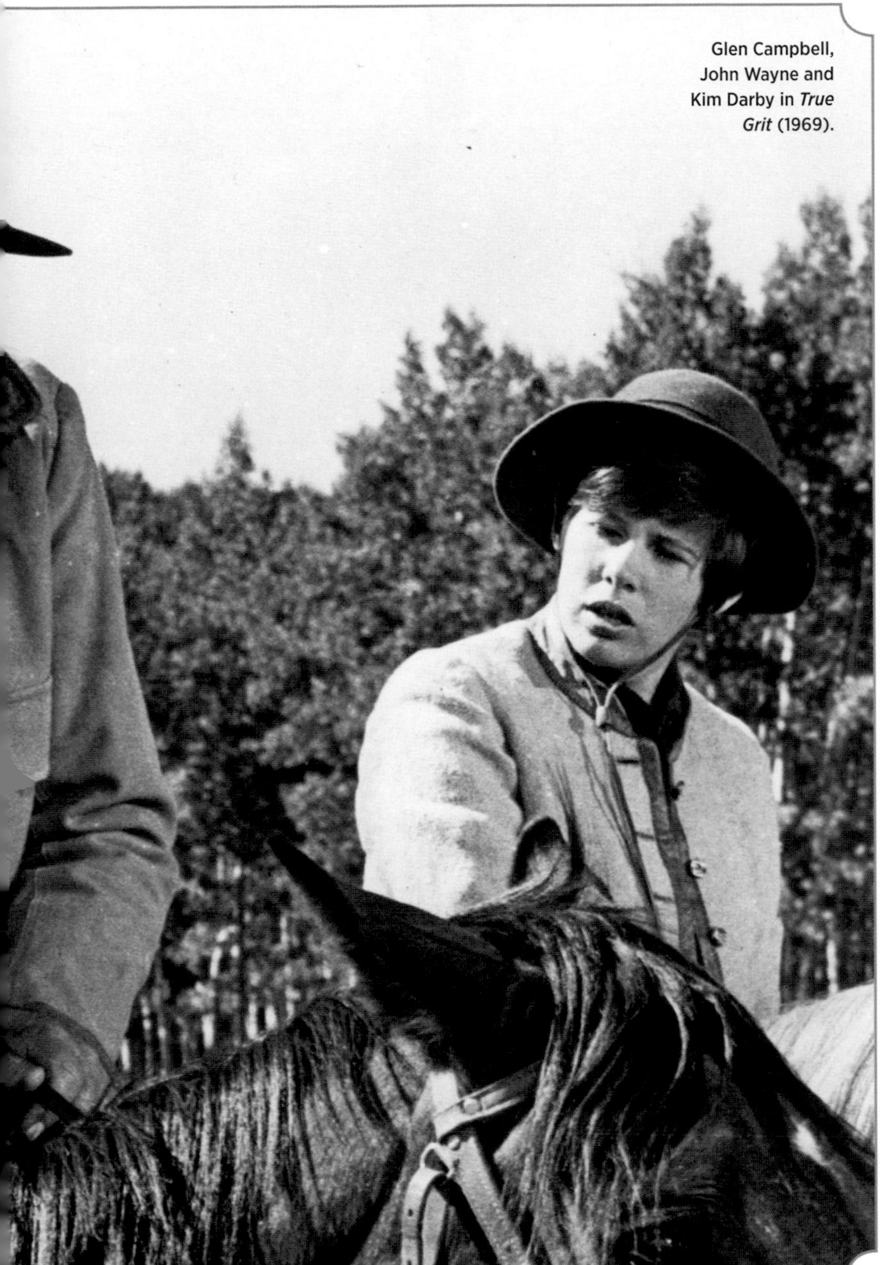

Glen Campbell, John Wayne and Kim Darby in *True Grit* (1969).

John Wayne as
J.B. Books in *The
Shootist* (1976).

REMEMBERING THE LEGEND

"One of the things that clearly differentiated him was that in his 70s, with nothing to prove, he was working as hard for the story and for the audience and for his own personal sense of self-respect probably as he ever had, maybe harder."

—RON HOWARD
from **John Wayne: The Legend and the Man**

"He worked that Colt Single Action Army revolver and became incredibly proficient with it. Harry Carey Jr. said to him on the set once, 'Jeez Duke, I didn't realize you were so good with a Colt!' And my father looked at him and replied, 'That's the dumbest thing I've ever heard you say.'"

—ETHAN WAYNE
Duke's youngest son

Duke and Emilio Fernández in a scene from *The War Wagon* (1967).

* GRIT *

"I don't like quitters."

—AS TOM DUNSON
Red River

n 1964, medical professionals informed Duke he had lung cancer, a diagnosis virtually tantamount to a death sentence at the time. Miraculously, the legend survived after having surgery to remove the cancer (along with one of his lungs and a few ribs). Most people would slow down and take it easy after such an ordeal. Not Duke. He was filming *The Sons of Katie Elder* less than a year after the surgery and continued making movies at his accustomed, rapid-fire pace until his death 15 years later.

ohn Wayne came up in the industry under the wing of mentors such as the great stuntman Yakima Canutt, and as a result he wasn't a stranger to performing dangerous stunts when making his films. In 1945's *Back to Bataan*, Duke rose to the challenge presented to him by director Edward Dmytryk and screenwriter Ben Barzman, who seemed to delight in crafting scenarios meant to have Duke cry "uncle!" They were disappointed. John Wayne accomplished feats of resilience that defied belief, including staying submerged in near-frozen water with only a flimsy reed to breath through.

John Wayne in *Back to Bataan* (1945).

★ GRIT ★

"Baby sister, I was born game, and I intend to go out that way."

—AS ROOSTER COGBURN
True Grit

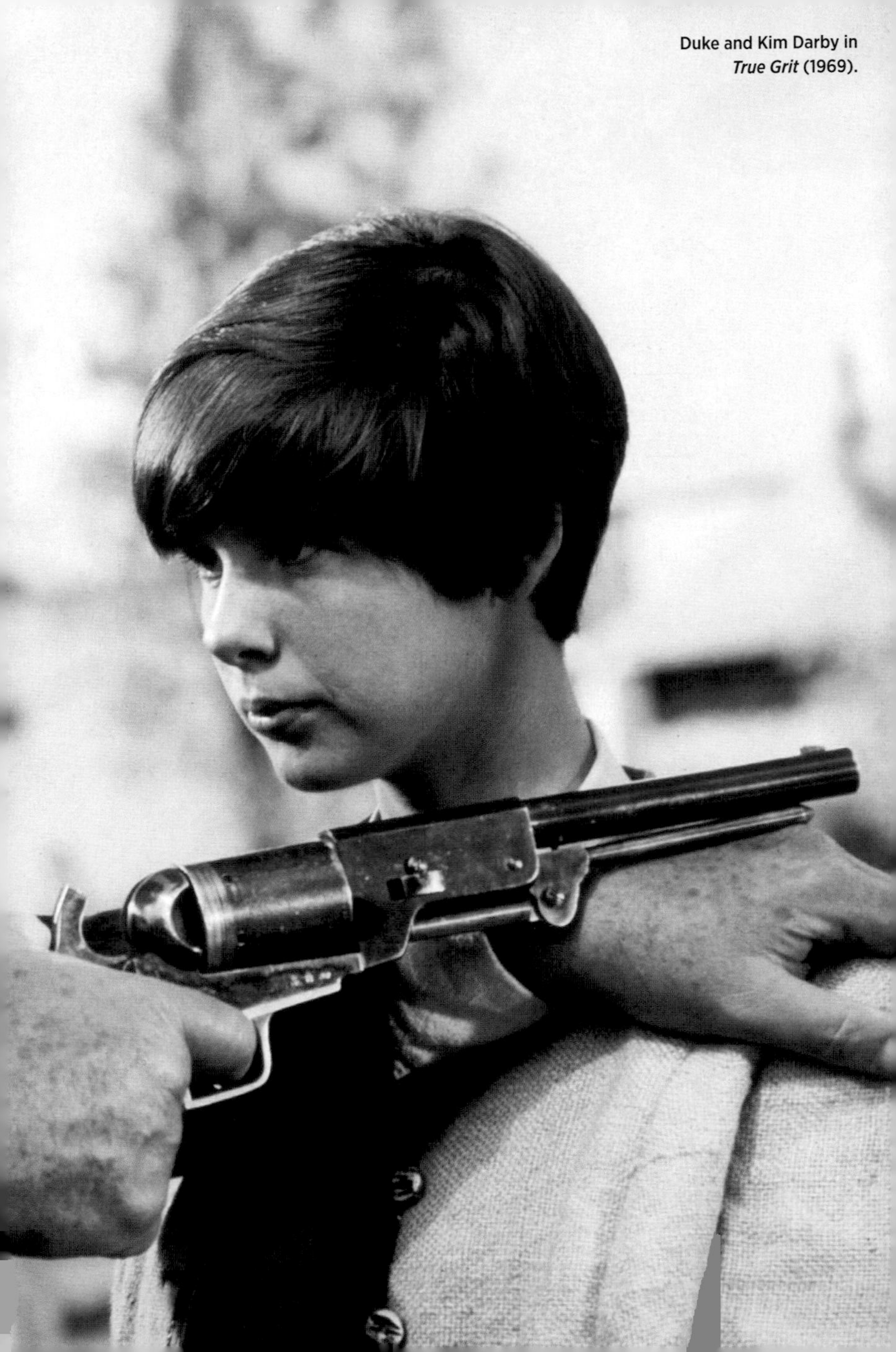

Duke and Kim Darby in *True Grit* (1969).

John Wayne and an American soldier share a laugh during the legend's trip to Vietnam.

★

hen American soldiers put their lives on the line for freedom in Southeast Asia, Duke made sure to journey to the frontlines to bolster the troops' spirits. While visiting Vietnam, John Wayne narrowly escaped an enemy sniper's bullet meant to end his life. The incident didn't faze the actor, who continued his tour and went home to make *The Green Berets,* his ode to the men carrying out America's mission.

★

f the many traits and values that propelled Duke to success, his grit was probably the main reason he became a Hollywood superstar. The young Duke was working part time as a propman at Fox Film Corporation to supplant the scholarship he received as a member of USC's football team when he caught the eye of director John Ford. Ford challenged Duke to drop into a three-point stance, and then promptly kicked the young man's hands out from under him. Undeterred, Duke got back up and told the director to give it another try. When John Wayne surprised Ford by knocking him down, the two men recognized the same spirit of grit in each other and a friendship was born.

Duke takes a
classic stance as
a member of the
USC football team.

John Wayne shares the screen with two of his costars in *The Big Trail* (1930). The film was the first time Duke was credited as "John Wayne."

GRIT

"When you stop fighting, that's death.

—AS BRECK COLEMAN
The Big Trail

"I define manhood simply: Men should be tough, fair and courageous— never petty, never looking for a fight, but never backing down from one either."

—JOHN WAYNE

John Wayne socks it to actor "Big" John Hamilton in a scene from *McLintock!* (1963).

John Wayne
in *The Horse
Soldiers* (1959).

"Kirby, you tangle with me, I'll have your hide."

—AS COL. JOHN MARLOWE
The Horse Soldiers

Duke in *Sands of Iwo Jima* (1949).

Patriotism

THE RED, WHITE AND BLUE
COURSED THROUGH DUKE'S VEINS.

John Wayne stands by the street sign honoring his name in Prescott, Arizona, while filming *El Dorado* (1966).

REMEMBERING THE LEGEND

"What my father loved best about America was the opportunity. He's the paradigm for the American Dream—available to everyone driven to succeed."

—PATRICK WAYNE
Duke's son

"To the people of the world, John Wayne is not just an actor—and a very fine actor—John Wayne is the United States of America...I beg you to strike a medal for Duke, to order the president to strike it. And I feel that the medal should say just one thing: 'John Wayne, American.'"

—MAUREEN O'HARA
to the U.S. Congress

John Wayne and
Maureen O'Hara in
Rio Grande (1951).

Duke celebrates with members of the American Hereford Association. John Wayne raised prize-winning Hereford cattle on his 26 Bar Ranch.

PATRIOTISM

"This is a good country, with good people in it."
—John Wayne

Marion Morrison (the name given to John Wayne at birth) as an infant.

"My dad came from very humble beginnings, and he really appreciated that if you were willing to do the work, you weren't guaranteed but you could become successful in America. He had a great love for this country."

—ETHAN WAYNE
Duke's youngest son

★

uring World War II, John Wayne dedicated himself to volunteering whatever spare time he had to the war effort, despite his responsibilities as both a Hollywood celebrity and a family man. Some of his contributions included serving up Thanksgiving turkeys at the Hollywood Canteen, going on tour with the USO and, most importantly, portraying the American serviceman with dignity, bravery and rectitude. Decades later, Duke continued to lift troops' spirits by visiting the frontlines of Vietnam, proving his lifelong commitment to America's soldiers.

Duke visits soldiers in Vietnam, 1966.

Duke at his home in Newport Beach, posing with his many accolades.

★ PATRIOTISM ★

"I do think we have a pretty wonderful country, and I thank God that He chose me to live here."

—JOHN WAYNE

John Wayne on the set of *The Shootist* (1976).

★

uke was such an outspoken American patriot during the Cold War that Soviet leader Joseph Stalin planned to have him assassinated in order to snuff out a shining example of individual liberty and freedom. This order would become a common thread throughout the communist world and would resurface during the Vietnam War, when Chinese leader Chairman Mao followed Stalin's lead in placing a bounty on Duke's head. Nikita Khrushchev later claimed he personally lifted the order.

Duke in *The Longest Day* (1962).

"Just give the American people a good cause, and there's nothing they can't lick."

—JOHN WAYNE

★

Moved by the sacrifice of American troops in Vietnam, John Wayne devoted his talent and energies to both boosting the morale of the soldiers abroad and telling their story to movie audiences back home. In addition to visiting the troops on the other side of the world, Duke put years of labor into making *The Green Berets* a reality. Though the film was considered a quixotic pursuit by some, Duke felt it was important to give the American people a realistic look at what their boys in uniform were doing to keep them safe. *The Green Berets* holds the honorable distinction of being the only film explicitly supporting the American mission in Vietnam while the conflict still raged.

Duke with son Patrick in a scene from *The Green Berets* (1968).

Duke and his son Patrick (bending over) with others at the 26 Bar Ranch.

The West—the very words go straight to that place of the heart where Americans feel the spirit of pride in their Western heritage.

—JOHN WAYNE

"My hope and prayer is that everyone know and love our country for what she really is and what she stands for."

—JOHN WAYNE

Duke in *The Cowboys* (1972).

Honesty

THE LEGEND ALWAYS CALLED IT HOW HE SAW IT.

Duke passes the time on the set of *Circus World* (1964) with a game of chess.

John Wayne and
Maureen O'Hara
in *The Quiet Man*
(1952).

"Speaking as an actress, I wish all actors would be more like Duke. And speaking as a person, it would be nice if all people could be honest and as genuine as he is."

—MAUREEN O'HARA
friend and frequent costar

Duke in *Hondo* (1953).

"A man oughta do what he thinks is right."

—AS HONDO LANE
Hondo

A young John Wayne (left) with his brother Robert and their father Clyde.

"I've always followed my father's advice: He told me, first, to always keep my word and, second, to never insult anybody unintentionally."

—JOHN WAYNE

REMEMBERING THE LEGEND

"John Wayne was bigger than life. In an age of few heroes, he was the genuine article."

—PRESIDENT JIMMY CARTER
39th President of the United States

Duke in *The War Wagon* (1967).

Duke and Robert Mitchum in *El Dorado* (1966).

"His gifted projection of the virtues of justice and equality, purpose and determination and forthright honesty have affected the American image all over the world. His living testimony to his spoken beliefs contributes respect to that image.... As a man, he has achieved his place with dignity."

—ROBERT MITCHUM
Hollywood actor and costar

ohn Wayne may have supported many prominent Republican politicians whose understanding of American values aligned with his own, but Duke's true allegiance was always to what he believed was right, and he wasn't shy in letting others know it. One prominent example of the actor's honesty was his adamant support of the Panama Canal Treaty, which many of Duke's conservative friends—including Ronald Reagan—stood against. Duke followed his conscience and wrote numerous letters to his acquaintances in politics letting them know his honest opinion. In recognition of Duke's brave and impassioned argument in favor of Panama, the country's president gifted John Wayne the island of Taborcillo lying just off the Central American nation's coast.

Duke signs autographs for fans. The actor would sometimes carry name cards he already had signed to make sure all his fans could receive his signature.

"You're going to think I'm being corny, but this is how I really feel: I hope my family and my friends will be able to say that I was an honest, kind and fairly decent man."
—JOHN WAYNE

Duke at Harvard
Square Theatre
in Cambridge,
Massachusetts,
January 15, 1974.

TRUE TALL TALES

★

In January 1974, John Wayne took up the gauntlet thrown down by editors of the left-leaning *Harvard Lampoon* and journeyed into the heart of liberal academia to accept the "Brass Balls" award. While everyone expected the rhetorical barbs aimed at Duke would reduce him to shambles, the actor's honesty won the crowd of 1,600 attendees over during the Q&A session. For example, when asked about the "phony toupee" he sometimes wore, Duke replied, "It's not phony. It's real hair. Of course, it's not mine, but it's real."

John Wayne in
The Comancheros
(1961).

"Words are what men live by...words they say and mean."

—AS JAKE CUTTER
The Comancheros

TRUE TALL TALES

Duke's legendary career resulted from not only the actor's hard work and magnetic screen presence, but also his ability to say "no" when a role offered wasn't right for him. In an industry rife with double-talk and insincere compliments, Duke was completely forthright with director Mel Brooks when the comedy genius offered John Wayne the part of "The Waco Kid" in the movie *Blazing Saddles*. According to Brooks, Duke read the script and told him the movie was too raunchy for him to star in, but he would be first in line to see it in the theater.

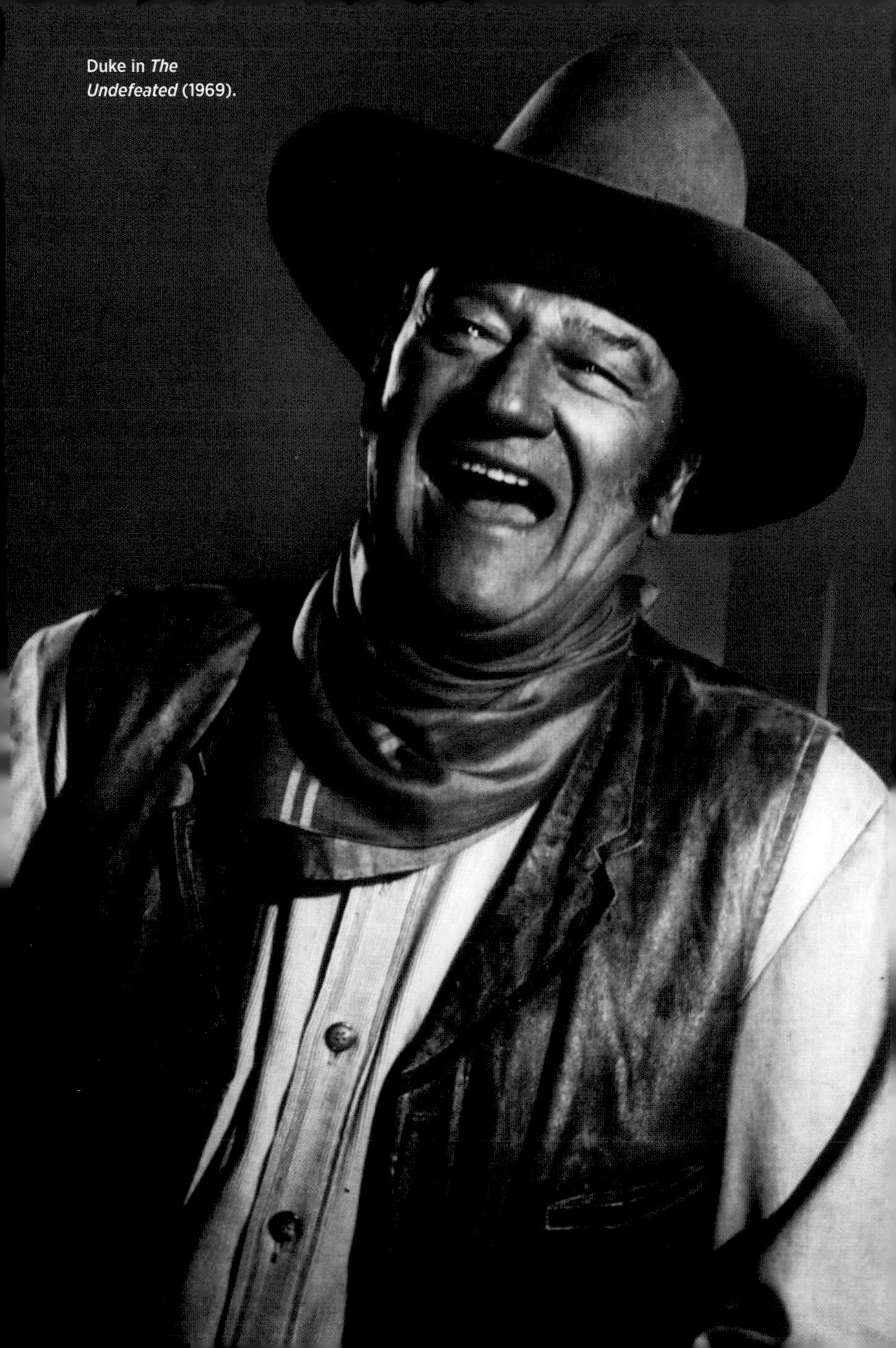

Duke in *The Undefeated* (1969).

"I suppose my best attribute, if you want to call it that, is sincerity. I can sell sincerity because that's the way I am."

—John Wayne

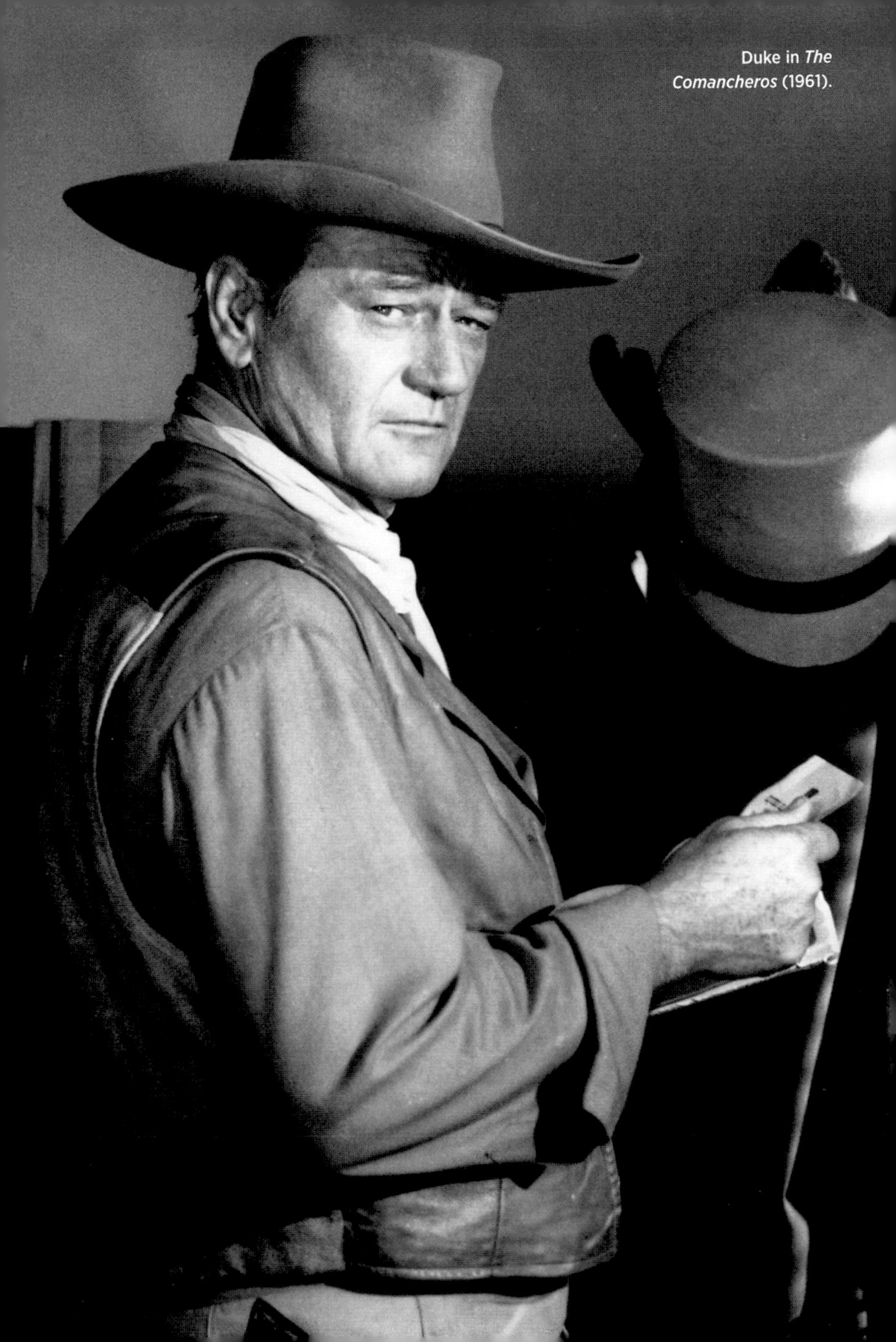

Duke in *The Comancheros* (1961).

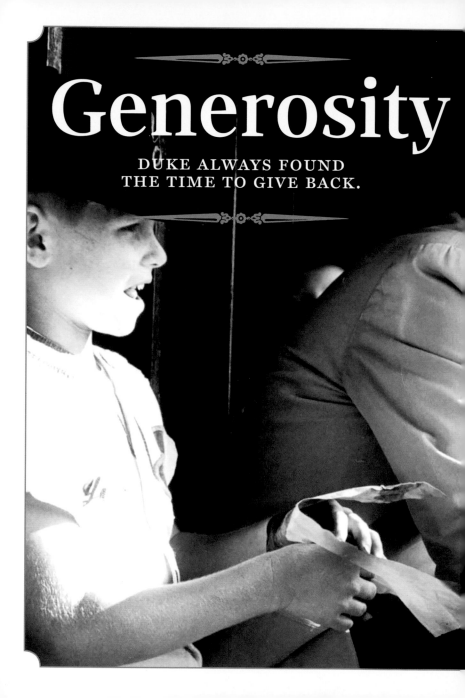

Generosity

DUKE ALWAYS FOUND
THE TIME TO GIVE BACK.

Duke in the dugout with one of the Little League teams he sponsored.

Duke hangs out with his mother, Mary Brown, on the set of *El Dorado* (1966).

"The greatest piece of advice my grandfather gave was to treat others the way you would want to be treated and to always be nice to my mother. Both pieces of advice have served me well all of my life."

—ANITA SWIFT
John Wayne's granddaughter

REMEMBERING THE LEGEND

"Duke got along with most people. He was so kind to me, he really and truly was. Doing as many films as I did with him, he was just a fine man. And he was fair. He said if you've got a problem let me hear it, and he says we'll take it from there. He was just great to work with."

—ED FAULKNER
Duke's friend and frequent costar

John Wayne and
Ed Faulkner on the
set of *The Green
Berets* (1968).

Duke hoists a lucky youngster while visiting Hawaii.

"I am a demonstrative man, a baby picker-upper, a hugger and a kisser—that's my nature."

—JOHN WAYNE

Duke holds his daughter Aissa on set of *The Alamo* (1960).

REMEMBERING THE LEGEND

"He lives his own life by strict rules and strict regulations, and he adheres to those things, those rules. He expects you, his friends, and you, his countrymen, to live by the same rules and to obey those rules. But then he has a very soft heart, and if you do make a mistake, he will bend those rules, not for himself, but to forgive you. And that is friendship and love."

—MAUREEN O'HARA
Duke's friend and frequent costar

As a beloved Hollywood icon, John Wayne received an inordinate amount of fan mail. While most celebrities of his stature might be tempted to ignore the piles of letters from admirers, Duke dove into the task with relish, answering as many missives as he could. He would spend hours corresponding with soldiers, boy scouts and regular fans who had taken the time to write to the larger-than-life role model. In John Wayne's mind, he owed everything to his fans—giving back a little portion of his day was the least he could do.

Duke poses for a photo with his adoring fans.

"A man deserves a second chance, but keep an eye on him."

—JOHN WAYNE

James Caan and
John Wayne in
El Dorado (1966).

Duke's son Patrick shows his father and a guest a calf at 26 Bar Ranch in Arizona.

uke wasn't just a cowboy on-screen. He managed cattle in real life, at his 26 Bar Ranch and the Red River Feedyard in Arizona. One of the people working at the feedyard with Duke's cattle was a young Temple Grandin, whose revolutionary and humane method of handling the animals was accepted by Duke and the managers in charge of the lot. The legend's open-mindedness and generosity helped Grandin launch a career that's changed how we raise and treat livestock today.

ohn Wayne's generosity wasn't limited to grand gestures meant to attract media attention but also extended into the unsung good deeds the man performed every day. Even before he was a household name and could afford to give a little more away, Duke was always finding ways of helping out his fellow man. For example, on the set of the 1938 Western *Red River Range*, Duke purposely flubbed a line at the end of the day to force a reshoot, ensuring that the behind-the-scenes crew received overtime pay.

Duke in *The Man Who Shot Liberty Valance* (1962).

Duke in *The Alamo* (1960) and the mug he gifted to the cast and crew of that film.

Duke in *The Cowboys* (1972) and the mug he gifted to the cast and crew of that film.

Duke in *The War Wagon* (1967) and the mug he gifted to the cast and crew of that film.

Duke in *Donovan's Reef* (1963) and the mug he gifted to the cast and crew of that film.

★

orking with an actor of John Wayne's talent and dedication was the dream of anyone involved in the entertainment industry, but Duke always took an extra step when wrapping up a project to make sure everyone knew how much he appreciated their hard work. Each crew member would receive a personal mug (with a design by Duke) bearing their name and well wishes from the star.

Duke and son
MIchael watch a
friend take a turn
at the grill.